Hotel

Also by Carl Adamshick

Birches

Receipt

Saint Friend

Curses and Wishes

Hotel

Carl Adamshick

Four Way Books
Tribeca

Library of Congress Cataloging-in-Publication Data

Names: Adamshick, Carl, 1969- author.
Title: Hotel / Carl Adamshick.
Description: New York : Four Way Books, [2021] |
Identifiers: LCCN 2021005294 | ISBN 9781945588877 (paperback)
Subjects: LCGFT: Poetry.
Classification: LCC PS3601.D399 H68 2021 | DDC 811/.6--dc23
LC record available at https://lccn.loc.gov/2021005294

This book is manufactured in the United States of America and printed on acid-free paper.

Four Way Books is a not-for-profit literary press. We are grateful for the assistance we receive from individual donors, public arts agencies, and private foundations.

This publication is made possible with public funds from the New York State Council on the Arts, a state agency.

NEW YORK STATE OF OPPORTUNITY. | Council on the Arts

PROUD MEMBER
[clmp]

We are a proud member of the Community of Literary Magazines and Presses.

Contents

Dance Card

Pornography

America Spring Picnic

Shift Drink

Cherries in the Snow

Dance Card

Everything remained in its time. Everything burned up far away.

—Joaquín Pasos, translated by David Shook

After the Election

I receive a letter from the future.
It assures me everything
will be fine, that you and I
will share a meal with friends,
that one of us will open a book,
read a soft passage concerned
with the body and we will all,
somehow, feel a little closer.
I crawl back beneath blankets.
Nothing disappears or goes away.
Clouds under the light rally.
I predict heavy rain in the headlights
of parked cars, the day as it is—
a record stuck in its ending.
Alone in the bed's thick shadow
I draft a truce with the world
that will forever remain unread
and unsigned. Silence reflecting
a kind of madness—looking
within the dim corridors of being.
And for what, to see the citizens
of a small city stalled for a moment
at dusk with the pain of certainty
etched on their faces.

Allegiance

The promise my mother made
was to finish her cigarette.
Under the trellis, she looked calm.
Trumpet flowers spotted
the pointy green leaves.
Married to the task,
loyal to the commitment,
nothing would stop her
from pulling the fire
closer to her throat.
We make our choices.
Her cotton shirt gathered
mist, gas quiet in its tank.
There is murder behind
everything and a forbidding
end waiting for us on a stump.
When are we people
who need no absolution,
who have no claim to absolve?

After the Inauguration

You turn toward the bedside table
like you're having a conversation
with one of the children.

Tax Day

Coffee, this morning, posed
its problems, presented
its difficulties.
My mind, displaced,
a negative balance
in the emotional bank.
In line at the post office
I didn't even know why
we were waiting together.
A sheet of stamps
depicting birds in winter
made you happy.
Moon in broad daylight.
A field of red under
closed eyes. So much doled
out in equal measures.
Now we are home
eating rice, pickled ginger
and little fish packed in oil.

Broadcast

How long must we live
before we see no difference
between history and walking,
between evening fitting
into the night sky
and the way light musses
beach grass? How long
before we realize
what we haven't heard is true?

Hypothetically

I was unaware war started.
I didn't want to work
or pay taxes, wanted to spend
my day compensated in love.
So I didn't know the war started.
I was only against my government.
I liked the coffee shops and taverns.
I didn't want to work or pay taxes.
I believed the trees in the park.
I had no idea what people
in the news were talking about
or if they shouldn't be talking
about something else.
My understanding of money
was small and didn't include blood.
I couldn't pick up a gun,
even if I was alone with my president,
even if he was tied to a chair
with a black canvas bag
over his head. I couldn't shoot.
No matter how much good
I thought it would do.

Police Dog

I'm trying to live here without rule—
family analogous to the state.
Mostly nothing is happening for me,
because of me. Really, I don't concern
anyone. An individual is the smallest
world, especially if it has no currency.
I walk into Union Station, see a police
dog wearing a yellow vest listening
to two men talk as it cools its ass
on the marble floor. I'm trying to not
go under. There are these policies
and laws and things I don't necessarily
care for or believe in. I guess, I mean,
don't abide by. And the dog—I think—
has the authority to arrest me. It's just
after Christmas. To celebrate another
year of service, there is a municipality
dance in an old ballroom downtown.
The dog and the other members in blue
wear their finest. I hear many tales.
The dog is married. The dog has parents
and children, bank account and college
fund, access to the cadastral map, macled
eyes and a barbed cock, isn't apologetic,
understands himself to be what he is,
and takes his own orders from on high.
I fear none of us are getting along.
At the dance, his name is written in every
slot of the dance card. There's not a dance
he's not dancing.

Witold's Worldview

If a stranger throws a pebble at you
it will cause you to steal a spoon.

Pornography

In a Jane Austen novel pornography is what happens after the wedding

Pornography

We see her from behind,
on her knees, her vulva
two inches from being
perfectly framed.
Zooming in, the whole screen
becomes ass.
Her anus, a circle of flesh
you could slide on
like a wedding ring.
Her mouth makes
a zero over the glans.
Her head bobs
like a pom-pom.
For minutes this woman
with a ponytail
throws her mouth
down a cock.
You can see the tiny soles
of her stilettos.
It's clear they have
never been worn,
that they have never
been outside.

Pornography

I simply can't believe
the man is willing
to stand there naked
with an erection,
can't believe he's willing
to bury his face
in a backside cleft
as we watch. He lowers
spit into the slightly
opened waxed hole.
I can't believe we
can watch as his tongue
cleans the exit wound
of consumption.

Pornography

We always close the drapes,
close them so if someone
walked up to the window
they couldn't find a crack
between the fabric and the frame.
We keep the volume low.
Can you see us watching
as a woman sinks her hand
into the top of an unbuttoned
pair of jeans, as she unhooks
her bra, removes it without
taking her printed-tee off,
her nipples stiffly pushing
the soft faded cotton?
The man lifting his shirt
past his head, then dropping
it next to his blue denim.
It's as if we are watching
ourselves become naked
with each other. I feel oddly
beautiful, knowing they
are us and that we are them—
each of us in our own room.
She has straddled his hips.
He has a hand around her
throat. It feels oddly beautiful
knowing they are watching,
that they are quietly sitting
in darkness, that our light
is funneling into their eyes.

Pornography

The paper is glossy.
The photo is of a woman
with her chin on her raised right knee.
Her left nipple covered with electrical
tape and a sheer burgundy silk.
Her other leg is straight,
truncated by the magazine,
a leather clutch between her thighs—
open like a set of parentheses.
The zipper at the top
a dangling gold clitoris.
Above her hair in light letters
Prada or Louis Vuitton.

Pornography

What I want is the whole week off,
a new car, a new-car-smell
all the time, to travel. When
I talk about how I love cooking
I want to be talking about restaurants,
how I am brought what I order
and don't have to clean up.
I want to tip with little thought,
a lawn that is taken care of.
I want to be seen when I am
there and when I am not there.

Pornography

This is our dance.
It is not sex
or the story of sex,
but a metaphor for work.
You may not believe this.
You may say it's real
and disgusting,
that the authenticity
of her mouth around
his testicles or his
fist in the ass
of a man coming
on a velvet cushion
cannot be called a metaphor
and, of course,
you would be right.

America Spring Picnic

How gently time collapses into poetry.

—Yannis Ritsos, translated by Paul Merchant

Offsite

A linguistic cloud
sky broken into tributaries
moonlight unmoving on the river

Shuttering proliferation of peacock feathers
half-spoked iridescent wheel
illiterate in every language but one

Been a long time since we fed horses
morning steam tangled in tall grass
front desk like a beaver's dam

Suitcase frothing over with clothes
two people played chess in the lobby
an elegy for passion

Waiting in line for a greyhound
poets introduce themselves
midnight comes and goes

Been a long time since we took piano
spring assiduously increases
multiplying everything by one

A friend of a friend interrupts a story
an editor's advances
not rape in the traditional sense

Waking in each other's arms
stretching
the azalea and chrysanthemum

Underwear was on the countertop
grief for one's own end
waiting in line for a breakfast sandwich

Trying to exhaust the possibilities
ungracious lights of the center
writers circling their books

Been a long time since we were poolside
little umbrella above ice
agreeing with whoever is talking

Elevator
fish in a basket
this isn't our floor

At the microphone
removed like a pig from its heart
never looked up from the book

It was getting early or late
waiting in line for the bathroom
people fall in love with those who listen

Two people play cribbage in the lobby
nobs
fifteen two fifteen four fifteen six

Drunk under the chandelier
pink-frosted chocolate cake doughnut
sweater inside out

Lamplight lingers on the sofa
thinking about the book
it's been meaning to read

Been a long time since we saw a matinee
fourteenth-floor curtains drawn
clouds gathered at their lek

America Spring Picnic

The news is on
with the sound off
coffin lid fitted with a peephole

The prisoners of the hunger strike
were making no difference
memory a perennial

Hornet nest in the small birdhouse
dry under the eaves
we stepped toward the festival

Arras of stars
campfire in the valley
sound of two beer cans opening

Clip of traffic due to accident
clip of whale released from captivity
dead phone

The eyes in the dream calcinate
and the hyacinth has an accent
we can't comprehend

Love begs the tongue to destroy
all the joined syllables
society has honored with pages

Foreign policy
brandishing the long beak of a seabird
fear sunders the blue egg from within

Pharmaceutical conference
update on shooting
honey in plastic bear-shaped bottle

The doctors who write prescriptions
listen to waves on the quay
some sunlight caught in a boat's sail

Young artichokes hidden
within the great leaves
wish it were a hat

The priests don vestments
stoups replenished before service
bright lilies on the chancel floor

The priests at the farmers market
blankets folded in trunks
America spring picnic

Sunday afternoon at Kelley Point Park
something awful has happened
behind a family of bushes

The boy holds a cigarette burn
in the tomb of his fist
another under his white collar

The boy holds an ear of corn
watches the slow ferris wheel
map of silence

Checking the weather for a city
where friends will be wed
rays of light bugs and botanicals

Commuters checking the score
checking for messages
in the business of getting home

The neighbors on their lawn
music swimming through screens
empty chairs dusk no table

The neighbors on their balcony
smoke cigarettes
under the coin of their mother's death

At noon shadows play chess
stones half-sunk in mud
light in the cottonwood sway

Placket

Alameda
hours of straight rain
not a god but something close

I know you can't stay long
the weather here bothers you
love struggling in the lament

Hydrangea behind window
past days eager to happen again
lined up

*

Rope in the wardrobe
not wings feathers
not feathers barbule hooklet

Brilliant curved needles
hanging champagne flute
dress form for a doll

I know you can't stay long
this silence falls from your mouth
opening built for a sleeve

*

Cocoon on a plate
worsted ladle swelling in bone broth
who's serving this

A dark gelatinous terrine
what looks like a lung
on a bed of dried twisted vetch

Please
whoever you are
bring a candle for the flame

*

Car wears a tarp
engine block hangs from an oak
rusted dehiscent sac

Jetted pocket
longing rendered reality useless
the pursuit of a man

Then the actual man
drug in the vein tendrils
moon infirmed in hydrogen waves

*

Don't know what it's like to be me
lake in the distance
how you might lack faith

Transient thing I am
awash in the ink of gender
terrified to enter my own privacy

I hear you sleeping
and the linden sounds different
butterflies in the nasturtium

*

Horizon with scar of light
gauze soaked in lavender and honey
faded film overlay

August saw the trees cut down
the funeral home demolished
wish we could role-play later

Scraps for the rag merchant
going back into our days
even there things change

*

Towers of indecision
arpeggios on a blue chord
don't know what it's like to be me

Ego of interlocking circles
brief recursive nature
buttonhole lined with green thread

Breath is a symptom
hair coils bark obsidian teeth
a little light in the vitrine

Shift Drink

Time comes into it.
Say it.   Say it.
The universe is made of stories,
not of atoms.

—Muriel Rukeyser

The Cardinal Club

I ask only to eventually die
and be forgotten,
to be taken out of calendric time.

I ask only to suffer,
to see day and night
and not understand the wind

and to find others
as uncertain as myself.

I ask that dusk in summer
be the way it has always been,

that planets, bright as pain,
come back undiminished.

I'm not sure how we bear it.
Life has been a second
billions of feet deep.

I've stayed too long
without changing,
forgot what it's like to be

at the Cardinal Club
having a drink with strangers—
dark in the present tense.

I feel I'm here solely to illustrate
what it will mean to be gone.

Two Things in a Day

Heard singing
in the church of absence

Later
wanted a bar napkin
to cover the years

Mistakes

My friend's child knows nothing,
hasn't been inundated with knowledge.

God no God or many Gods
she can't ask.

She looks at a petunia,
she listens through a night screen—
don't tell her it's crickets.

Not yet—maybe not ever.

Bright in the park—hot slide.
Shouldn't I figure out
why my father hid his life
within my mother
like she was a closet

before I know why the sky
was cut and divided into the zodiac?

Advice—who knows?
If I took my own,
my questions wouldn't have any words.

The Relations We Have

Looking at a scale of geologic time
is humbling.

What I did today is pretty much
what I did yesterday
and what I'll do tomorrow.

Something else
emerged from the cocoon.
The caterpillar made its bed.

Love made its bed.

Neither of us knowing the cause
or the reason for the cause.

The pyramids are built.

We wake, more or less,
at the same hour,
see the same sunset,

hand our contingent perspectives
to one another.

We learn to fly.

Statements seem impossible.
I guess it's about choice—
the physics of choice.

We wear yoga pants
to the café or ratty shirts
with band names
and tour dates.

Some of us like mayonnaise.
Some science. Others believe
nothing. Luck is a naked emissary

carrying a silver tray
lined with knives
through the kitchen
into the backyard.

Hotel

If you remember anything
from this book
let it be

to read Grace Paley's
first poem in her first collection
of poems or *In the Bus*

or to find a friend
and take turns reading aloud
Speck's Idea by Mavis Gallant

or to chop onions
and tomatoes
while tuned to a station

where you can listen
to Eudora Welty's
Why I Live at the P.O.

Cold Pizza and a Cup of Coffee

Well
they published his diary
and I was rude enough to read it
Unlike most novels
people disappeared from the narrative
decades passed
those early friends were entirely gone

Jill and Josey Explain The Sullivan Nod

We are in a bar. We love bars—
summer, laughing in a corner

horseshoe booth. They are talking
about the accidental discovery of cider.

Well Josey is.
Jill runs golden-throated commentary.

Then we are on to The Sullivan Nod
and the finer elements of service.

As for the other patrons—
none of us knew one another
and it remained that way.

Horseradish

i

All winter the tree
in the courtyard leafless
Yellow at the bottom

of the tulip's cup
Night in the kitchen
Béchamel

Holsteins at the trough
Cold burr of the mill
What it takes

to accompany loneliness

ii

A well-made bed
before breakfast
is a sign of forgetting

Spring seems to prove
there is no end
Garbage

non-specific trash
clumps on the beach
or escaped from bags

along a woodland trail

iii

Lint
Our grand and silly
efforts in phonetics

The lemon glaze poured
on the bundt cake
looks like semen

but it's the shrimp
attracting attention
Bowl of tails

Whiskey sodas and chardonnay

Aubade

If you would have stayed
we could have had
my favorite breakfast

toast
peas
an egg over easy

coffee
We could have worked
on a letter to Frau Borchers

or I could have watched
you dress for a thousand years
and by then

you would have
an enormous white fur hat
and say something

very bossy to me
in Russian

Summer Salt

A mint julep
then the nape of your neck

Monday

Months and months can go by
before my daughter calls
while on a walk
I can be washing chard
and have to dry my hands
before handling the phone
It's like I'm in the backyard again
the sky empty of clouds
my father inside watching golf
eating pickled herring on crackers
my mother out searching
for something small for the house
What am I doing back there
I don't seem to be doing anything

Low Tide

I want these cigarettes
to kill you and sometimes
I think you do too.
So all the times outside
of parties and on porches
were not wasted.
How often have I seen
you unzip the pocket
of a dark-blue Cordura
Jansport and grab a pack
of American Spirits?
You quit—can't quit.
In the park at twenty,
Thanksgiving walks,
reprieves from family,
contemplative moments,
sentences for poems—
every lit page, drawn deeply
into life. Smoke ushering you
slowly into the realm
of your brother. King. Boy.
You are on both sides
of the mountain. If this
cigarette is your guide
next time you are on
the sands of low tide
please ask it to show you
the horse you can not see.

Colorado

My dream lives close to my lungs.
Sometimes I feel it as a pen
spilling ink in the dark purse
of my breathing. My body
lives here in Colorado,
in an apartment with a few plants.
I am what the experts refer to
as history, a small totality
making its way to the future.
In the evening, I inherit death
as an idea, as a subject I'll be tested on.
Mid-afternoons, I take long walks.
I live by myself as the state lives
by itself in borders it had nothing
to do with. I, too, have a river.
If you ask, I'll tell you all about the light.

Nightcap

It's so good now
There's no need to remember

Everything still exists
lakeshore litter
feelings

I haven't wanted to say
because of how I was raised
and because of the clover

the fogged streetlamps tucked in maples
but it's horrible here

In my self-portrait
I will not be at the canvas

As for the symbolism and placement
of objects I will wear
a dark gray-blue cloud
a great frock coiled like an ear or waves

an apricot on a twig with two leaves
will be stuck through the lapel

I'm having such fun
Let's have a string to tie it
two strings

Cherries in the Snow

for Kate

I can't say enough about this—red because sore
& polished because wet

—Fanny Howe

Cherries in the Snow

Speaking of Sylvia Plath
with lit Turkish Royal unspooling
in the pits of our lungs

I craved her. I wanted to live
in the long, soft revolution of her mouth,
to sleep and wake in the heat of its coup.

I know no one of her stature.
Her lipstick on the filter, the napkin,
on the glass of beer

bright as a candied clot of hemoglobin.
Revlon four-forty, she explained,
was Plath's go-to.

I tried to watch everything,
to be aware of what survived
behind each gesture—what fine raiment

still hung in her closet, what voile slip
or chiffon bandeau I might see.

She began telling me something
she didn't want me to know—
again and again lifting the cigarette

to the open forest of her face.

I began wondering what existed.
My cock knocking against the cloth
of my pants, clenching and unclenching

like a baby's fist at the breast of its mother.
Memory is our god,
the watcher lurking in the burnt
figure the tree lays on the grass.

She said bees—Sylvia wrote about bees.
So I knew bees were real.

The moon dug itself into clouds—
her nails, too, were Cherries in the Snow.

Hit and gaslit she stares into the heath—
a book without her name.

Two children
concealed in a game of dormition.

Surely this isn't happening—
gorse unmoving in the wind.

Nature's mask softens,
yew trees reveal garnets
set in the warlock's face—

enough melancholy to arouse a plague.
Gossip and hearsay, rumor and artifice
pack their bags.

No me No me No me

The shelves and teacups fade.
The whole of Court Green dissolves.

Her eyes burn through the fog
trying to see beyond
to the real day

where the sun lies on sand
and a family picnics.

Where is the dissembler,

the vain impregnator; his tower of words—
grimed machicolations.

Nothing is here except the night

they heard the bellwether
carrying love through November's slaughters.

To begin again—to find the world
without other meaning,
without men, after
the wreckage of not living.

It doesn't work that way for me
with just the mouth, she said.

She said, on the walk home,
night handed me the key
to its childhood.

Her screwback earrings
are on my nightstand.

They are red—the size of a holly berry.

I clasp one with its gold mechanics
on the lobe of my ear.

I want to be naive but not a child.
Also, I want to be a child and not naive.

I look, again, at the picture she sent.

From bed I hear things
being tossed about and swaying.

Her purple t-shirt hangs on the bedpost.

She's hunting sorrel
and chanterelle with your father.

I think of how she might think
of decay—hare skull, leaf rot
on a spat, centipedes

darting through the wet undergrowth.

I imagine a snail's vulnerable body,
butter and garlic
for the egg, some delicate green,
a brown cold withered bloom—

how tomorrow
I could remove the chipped polish
from her fingers and brush
each nail with a shimmery sea foam

lacquer she might push
into the darkness of my body.

I'd like to tell you again about yesterday.

It started like many others—
blue, white, calescent.

In the evening neighbors
talked on stoops and earlier
children didn't feel the need

to help clean dishes after dinner.

That's how it was.
Trillium remained silent—

stars tapped on the door.

My life one long run-on sentence
in the past tense

where the planished moon
and sounds of freight yards
ignite in a shadowy fire.

All the waking hours passed.
All the summers condensed.

Another succession of vowels
strikes the platen—

book as debridement.

Early dark mirror,
the intervals between
herself and her self—

tempered, mathematically divided.
Heaven being

a noun for death—an octave below
and the devil

on the board
casting his little, sarcastic vote.

Hooves hidden in hands,

wolf tone,
reverie of a Christmas farthingale—
yards of threaded gold,

a thousand embroidered
diamonds—silver, pearl and brume.

Resident in the precinct of winter,
dead frozen pollens
puncture and flurry

in the corner
where the light
is still on—lullaby of defeat,

a particular way
of approaching an outfit—

making and making, composing

until she is the scar
her mother left on the earth.

She said, a tongue
riffling my nipple can make me sad.
She said, trash fire—

I can't really do much without her voice.

The sky is ruched—pink to scarlet,
floating like a bloom of jellyfish.

My first and last body lies waiting
in the basement of its frustration—
anguish wears a stone.

Didn't Sylvia write: winter is for women,
didn't she want tiger pants?

Creation is a place of upheaval
and unrest. The mind much wilder

than reality—what happens there
never happens
until it happens.

She was here yesterday

wearing the diaphanous purple
of her inheritance, the garment
she unwillingly accepted.

Measly flakes drifted—not sticking.

Evening. Ash from her hand-rolled shag
slept in an upturned beer cap.

The bright blink
of the ambulance in the middle
of the street—

its lights, their specific
rotation and flash,

every so often,
caused the stop sign to appear blue.

Acknowledgments

Academy of American Poets, Love's Executive Order, American Poetry Review, and *Miracle Monocle.*

Carl Adamshick's first book received the Walt Whitman Award from the Academy of American Poets. His most recent collection, *Birches*, was published by Four Way Books. He writes an on-going article on etymology for the quarterly *Kitchen Table* called "A Word from the Kitchen." He lives in Portland, Oregon.

Publication of this book was made possible by grants and donations. We are also grateful to those individuals who participated in our 2020 Build a Book Program. They are:

Anonymous (14), Robert Abrams, Nancy Allen, Maggie Anderson, Sally Ball, Matt Bell, Laurel Blossom, Adam Bohannon, Lee Briccetti, Therese Broderick, Jane Martha Brox, Christopher Bursk, Liam Callanan, Anthony Cappo, Carla & Steven Carlson, Paul & Brandy Carlson, Renee Carlson, Cyrus Cassells, Robin Rosen Chang, Jaye Chen, Edward W. Clark, Andrea Cohen, Ellen Cosgrove, Peter Coyote, Janet S. Crossen, Kim & David Daniels, Brian Komei Dempster, Matthew DeNichilo, Carl Dennis, Patrick Donnelly, Charles Douthat, Morgan Driscoll, Lynn Emanuel, Monica Ferrell, Elliot Figman, Laura Fjeld, Michael Foran, Jennifer Franklin, Sarah Freligh, Helen Fremont & Donna Thagard, Reginald Gibbons, Jean & Jay Glassman, Ginny Gordon, Lauri Grossman, Naomi Guttman & Jonathan Mead, Mark Halliday, Beth Harrison, Jeffrey Harrison, Page Hill Starzinger, Deming Holleran, Joan Houlihan, Thomas & Autumn Howard, Elizabeth Jackson, Christopher Johanson, Voki Kalfayan, Maeve Kinkead, David Lee, Jen Levitt, Howard Levy, Owen Lewis, Jennifer Litt, Sara London & Dean Albarelli, David Long, James Longenbach, Excelsior Love, Ralph & Mary Ann Lowen, Jacquelyn Malone, Donna Masini, Catherine McArthur, Nathan McClain, Richard McCormick, Victoria McCoy, Ellen McCulloch-Lovell, Judith McGrath, Debbie & Steve Modzelewski, Rajiv Mohabir, James T. F. Moore, Beth Morris, John Murillo & Nicole Sealey, Michael & Nancy Murphy, Maria Nazos, Kimberly Nunes, Bill O'Brien, Susan Okie & Walter Weiss, Rebecca Okrent, Sam Perkins, Megan Pinto, Kyle Potvin, Glen Pourciau, Kevin Prufer, Barbara Ras, Victoria Redel, Martha Rhodes, Paula Rhodes, Paula Ristuccia, George & Nancy Rosenfeld, M. L. Samios, Peter & Jill Schireson, Rob Schlegel, Roni & Richard Schotter, Jane Scovell, Andrew Seligsohn & Martina Anderson, James & Nancy Shalek, Soraya Shalforoosh, Peggy Shinner, Dara-Lyn Shrager, Joan Silber, Emily Sinclair, James Snyder & Krista Fragos, Alice St. Claire-Long, Megan Staffel, Bonnie Stetson, Yerra Sugarman, Dorothy Tapper Goldman, Marjorie & Lew Tesser, Earl Teteak, Parker & Phyllis Towle, Pauline Uchmanowicz, Rosalynde Vas Dias, Connie Voisine, Valerie Wallace, Doris Warriner, Ellen Doré Watson, Martha Webster & Robert Fuentes, Calvin Wei, Bill Wenthe, Allison Benis White, Michelle Whittaker, and Ira Zapin.